KYLER MURRAY

SUPERSTAR

BY WILL GRAVES

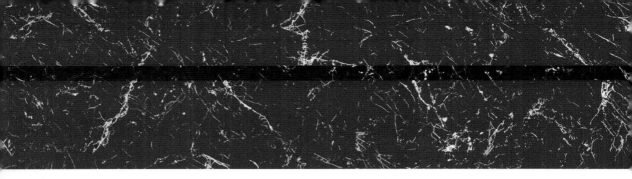

First Edition
First Printing, 2019

Book design by Jake Nordby
Cover design by Jake Nordby
Photographs ©: Matt York/AP Images, cover, 1, back cover; Jeff Chiu/AP Images, 4; Alonzo Adams/AP Images, 7, 25; Michael Prengler/Cal Sport Media/AP Images, 8; LM Otero/AP Images, 11, 22; Mike Janes/Four Seam Images/AP Images, 13; Patrick Green/Cal Sport Media/AP Images, 14; Max Faulkner/Star-Telegram/AP Images, 17; Sue Ogrocki/AP Images, 19; James D. Smith/AP Images, 21; Jeffrey McWhorter/AP Images, 20–21, 30; Mark Humphrey/AP Images, 27; Red Line Editorial, 29

Press Box Books, an imprint of Press Room Editions.

Library of Congress Control Number: 2019940212

ISBN
978-1-63494-133-4 (library bound)
978-1-63494-134-1 (paperback)
978-1-63494-136-5 (epub)
978-1-63494-135-8 (hosted ebook)

Distributed by North Star Editions, Inc.
2297 Waters Drive
Mendota Heights, MN 55120
www.northstareditions.com

Printed in the United States of America

About the Author

Will Graves serves as correspondent for The Associated Press in Pittsburgh, where he covers the NHL, the NFL, and Major League Baseball, as well as various Olympic sports.

TABLE OF CONTENTS

9/25/19
$9.95

CHAPTER 1

Dual Threat 5

CHAPTER 2

Following His Father 9

CHAPTER 3

Super Sooner 15

CHAPTER 4

Going Pro 23

Timeline • 28
At-a-Glance • 30
Glossary • 31
To Learn More • 32
Index • 32

#RootedInOakland
@athletics
OAKLAND ATHLETICS
A's
A's
50
2018
athletics.com
athletics.com

1 DUAL THREAT

Kyler Murray knew at some point he'd have to choose between playing baseball and playing football. A mistake in setting his alarm clock might have made the decision for him.

In the summer of 2018, Murray's future looked to be in baseball. He had barely seen the field as a college quarterback. And the Oakland Athletics liked the hard-throwing, hard-running outfielder so much they picked him ninth overall in the Major League Baseball (MLB) draft.

The Oakland Athletics were ready for Kyler Murray to become a big part of their organization.

The A's even said Murray could go back to the University of Oklahoma for his senior football season. Murray finally became the Sooners' starting quarterback. The first month of the season went by quietly. Then Murray was late to practice one day, breaking a team rule. He told coach Lincoln Riley he hadn't set the right time on his alarm clock. It didn't matter.

Riley benched Murray for the start of the next game as punishment, only bringing him in after the first possession.

Eager to make it up to Riley, Murray made the most of his time against Baylor. He passed for 432 yards and six touchdowns. He

WHY NOT BOTH?

A handful of athletes have played in both the NFL and MLB. Running back Bo Jackson did it in the 1980s. Then cornerback Deion Sanders did it in the 1990s. However, that was never really an option for Murray. That's because the quarterback position is so demanding in the NFL.

Murray's big game against Baylor helped kickstart his dominant senior season.

also ran for a score in a 66–33 win. His success continued for the rest of the season. Murray led the Sooners to the Big 12 Conference title and a spot in the College Football Playoff. He won the Heisman Trophy as the top player in college football. And then he really had a decision to make. Was his future in MLB? Or was he going to try his luck in the National Football League (NFL)?

2 FOLLOWING HIS FATHER

Kyler Murray was born on August 7, 1997, in Bedford, Texas. Playing two sports was in his blood. His dad, Kevin, was also skilled in baseball and football. The Milwaukee Brewers even drafted Kevin, and he played a year in the minor leagues. However, he decided to play quarterback at Texas A&M instead.

Kevin Murray never made it to the majors or the NFL. But he still passed down his love for both sports to his son.

Even when Kyler was in high school, his talent on the football field was obvious.

Like his dad, Kyler quickly stood out from the crowd. He became Allen High School's starting quarterback six games into his sophomore season. And he never looked back. Kyler started 43 games for Allen. The Allen Eagles walked off the field victorious after all 43. Three times Kyler led the team to the state title game. Three times the Eagles were crowned state champions.

One of Kyler's best games came against mighty DeSoto High. The teams met in a 2013 playoff game. Allen trailed 35–20 in the fourth quarter. Fans started to leave. They figured Allen's unbeaten run was over.

Not so fast. Kyler started Allen's rally with a 68-yard touchdown pass. He finished it off with a 24-yard touchdown run in the final seconds. Allen triumphed 42–35.

Kyler escapes from a Cypress Ranch defender during the 2014 Texas 6A high school state championship game.

The teams met again in the 2014 playoffs. This time Kyler did the damage with his legs. He scored three rushing touchdowns. He also helped set up the game-winning field goal. Allen won 25–22. The Eagles went on to win the state championship for a third straight year.

Kyler finished his senior season with 54 passing touchdowns. He added 25 more on the ground. Several organizations even named him national high school football player of the year.

For most athletes, being great at one sport would be enough. Not for Kyler. He proved to be just as dangerous on the baseball diamond. At 5 feet 10 inches and 180 pounds, he could hit for power. He also had plenty of speed on the base paths. Plus, he had a rocket for a right arm.

Kyler graduated in 2015. Many baseball scouts considered him to be a top prospect. But Kyler had other ideas. He told MLB

DOUBLE TROUBLE

The clothing company Under Armour hosts games for top high school athletes. They are kind of like all-star games. As a senior, Kyler played in both the football and baseball games. No player had done that before.

Kyler showed off his baseball skills at the 2014 Under Armour All-America Game at Wrigley Field in Chicago.

teams not to draft him. He planned to follow in his dad's footsteps and play quarterback at Texas A&M. As Kyler soon learned, though, life doesn't always go according to plan.

3 SUPER SOONER

Texas A&M fans got a preview of what Kyler Murray could become in the fall of 2015. The freshman quarterback threw for 686 yards and five touchdowns. However, he saw a brighter future elsewhere. So he decided to transfer to Oklahoma. He liked the team's offensive coordinator, Lincoln Riley. Murray thought he and Riley would work well together.

College rules forced Murray to sit out all of 2016. He spent most of 2017 watching, too. That's because Oklahoma

Murray showed promise during his lone season at Texas A&M.

already had a great starting quarterback in Baker Mayfield. He won that year's Heisman Trophy.

Murray stayed plenty busy at Oklahoma. He joined the baseball team as an outfielder in 2017. By the following spring he became a starter. His numbers took off, too. Murray hit .296 with 10 home runs in 2018. He also added 10 stolen bases.

The Oakland Athletics had seen enough. That summer, they selected Murray with the ninth pick in the 2018 MLB Draft. Murray signed with the team. His contract included a $4.66 million signing bonus. But he didn't join the other draftees in heading to the minor leagues. Instead, Murray returned to Oklahoma.

By then, Riley had become the Sooners' head coach. Mayfield was gone, too. With

Teammate Steele Walker (1) congratulates Murray on a home run for the Sooners.

Murray in the starter's role, the Sooners hit their stride. Week after week, their games followed a similar pattern. The defense had trouble stopping opponents. But Murray was so good it didn't matter.

Oklahoma averaged 48.4 points per game in 2018. That was the most out of the 130 teams

BETTERING BAKER

Baker Mayfield was a record-setting quarterback at Oklahoma. In many ways, Murray did Mayfield one better. He became the second player ever to pass for 4,000 yards and rush for 1,000 yards in the same season. His passer rating of 199.2 also beat Mayfield's school record of 198.9 set the year before.

in major college football. Murray did most of the damage. He threw for 42 touchdowns and ran for 12 more.

The Sooners met the rival Texas Longhorns in the Big 12 Conference title game. Texas had been the only team to beat Oklahoma that season. The teams were tied heading into the fourth quarter. That's when Murray flashed some more magic. He threw the clinching touchdown pass with two minutes left in the game. The Sooners were conference champions.

One week later, Murray was all smiles in New York City after winning the Heisman Trophy.

Finally in a starting role, Murray thrived as Oklahoma's quarterback in 2018.

Not bad for a guy who had already signed a professional baseball contract, right? Turns out, Murray wasn't going to be a Major League Baseball player after all.

BIG-TIME THROW

Murray's 40th touchdown pass in 2018

18-yard pass to Grant Calcaterra

Firing his third touchdown pass of the day

The Sooners were tied with Texas going into the fourth quarter of the 2018 Big 12 Conference title game. Then Murray went to work, hitting a tightly covered Grant Calcaterra in stride for the clinching touchdown in a 39–27 victory. Many believed this performance sealed Murray's rise to become the seventh Sooner to win the Heisman Trophy.

Kyler Murray
University of Oklahoma

4 GOING PRO

Kyler Murray had one last college football game. The Sooners met Alabama on December 29 as part of the College Football Playoff. Fresh off winning the Heisman, Murray was spectacular. He threw for 308 yards and rushed for 109 against the toughest defense in the country. However, Alabama won 45–34.

The game was supposed to be Murray's last on a football field. The Athletics figured Murray would now focus on baseball. But Murray had second

Murray won the 2018 Davey O'Brien Award as the top college quarterback.

thoughts. After playing both sports for so many years, it was time to choose. Unfortunately for the Athletics, Murray picked football. A few days before Murray was supposed to report to spring training with the A's, he announced he would enter the NFL Draft instead.

The decision was a risky one for Murray. The risk had nothing to do with his ability. Anyone who had ever played against him knew he could play. Instead, Murray's challenge was convincing NFL teams he was tall enough to succeed. Some NFL teams worried Murray wouldn't be big enough to see over his offensive line.

Murray did his best to prove he could do the job. He joined other top prospects at the NFL Scouting Combine before the draft. He measured 5 feet 10 inches. That is one inch

Murray's pre-draft workouts proved to NFL scouts that he was the real deal.

shorter than Seattle Seahawks quarterback Russell Wilson. Wilson's height didn't stop him. He led the 2013 Seahawks to a Super Bowl title in only his second NFL season. Murray was determined to not let his height stop him either.

NFL scouts came out to Oklahoma to watch Murray again. This time Murray showed off his powerful arm. He completed 61 of 67 passes, showing the same kind of zip on the ball that had impressed his teammates at Allen High years earlier. Before long the question was not whether Murray would be a first-round pick, but whether he would be the first overall pick.

As the draft got closer, that possibility began to feel like more of a certainty. Finally, on April 25, 2019, the wait was over.

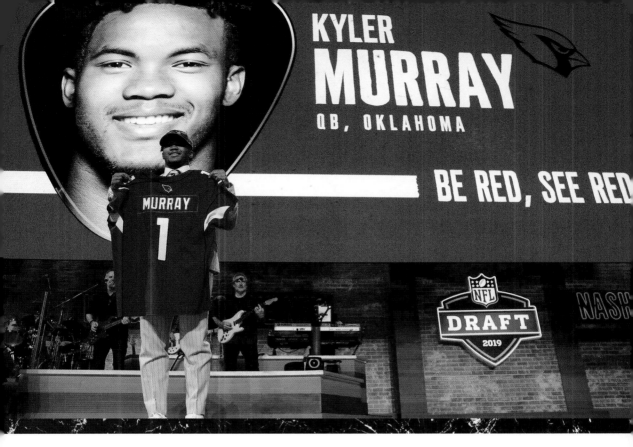

Murray became the first player to be selected in the first round of both the MLB and NFL drafts.

NFL commissioner Roger Goodell walked to the podium and announced that the Arizona Cardinals had selected Murray with the first pick.

"This is a dream come true," Murray said. And that dream was only just beginning.

TIMELINE

1. ## Bedford, Texas (August 7, 1997)
   Kyler Murray is born.

2. ## Arlington, Texas (2014)
   Murray leads Allen High School to a third straight Texas state football championship.

3. ## Houston, Texas (September 5, 2015)
   Murray makes his college football debut for Texas A&M.

4. ## Norman, Oklahoma (2016)
   Murray transfers to Oklahoma in the fall.

5. ## Norman, Oklahoma (February 24, 2018)
   Murray hits his first home run for the Oklahoma baseball team in an 11-4 loss to Valparaiso.

6. ## Oakland, California (June 4, 2018)
   The Oakland Athletics select Murray with the ninth overall pick in the 2018 MLB draft.

7. ## New York, New York (December 8, 2018)
   Murray becomes the seventh Oklahoma football player to win the Heisman Trophy.

8. ## Glendale, Arizona (April 25, 2019)
   Murray joins the Arizona Cardinals after they select him with the first pick in the NFL Draft.

MAP

Birth date: August 7, 1997

Birthplace: Bedford, Texas

Position: Quarterback

Throws: Right

Height: 5 feet 10 inches

Weight: 207 pounds

Current team:
Arizona Cardinals
(2019–)

Past teams: Texas A&M
Aggies (2015), Oklahoma
Sooners (2017–2018)

Major awards: Heisman Trophy (2018), Davey O'Brien Award (2018),
All-American (2018), Big 12 Offensive Player of the Year (2018),
Gatorade National High School Football Player of the Year (2014).

Accurate through the 2018 season.

GLOSSARY

bonus
A one-time payment a player receives from his team.

combine
An event in which football players come together to show off their skills for NFL scouts.

commissioner
The person in charge of running a sports league.

contract
An agreement between a player and his team that states how much he will be paid and for how long.

draft
A process in which teams choose new players to add to their rosters.

minor league
The lower levels in which pro baseball players develop their skills.

prospect
An up-and-coming player who could someday reach the major leagues.

scout
A person who rates the ability of athletes. Scouts usually work for professional sports teams.

transfer
To switch schools.

TO LEARN MORE

Books

Chandler, Matt. *Football: A Guide for Players and Fans*. North Mankato, MN: Capstone Press, 2019.

Editors of Sports Illustrated Kids. *The Greatest Football Teams of All Time*. New York: Time Inc. Books, 2018.

Graves, Will. *Football Season Ticket: The Ultimate Fan Guide*. Mankato, MN: Press Box Books, 2019.

Websites

Arizona Cardinals Official Site
www.azcardinals.com

Murray's College Stats
www.sports-reference.com/cfb/players/kyler-murray-1.html

NFL Official Site
www.nfl.com

INDEX

Alabama, 23

Allen High School, 10–11, 26

Arizona Cardinals, 26–27

College Football Playoff, 7, 23

Heisman Trophy, 7, 16, 18, 21, 23

Kingsbury, Kliff, 26

Mayfield, Baker, 16, 18

Murray, Kevin, 9–10, 13

NFL Draft, 24, 26–27

Oakland Athletics, 5–6, 16, 23–24

Riley, Lincoln, 6, 15, 16

Rosen, Josh, 26

Texas A&M, 9, 13, 15

University of Oklahoma, 6–7, 15–19, 26

Wilson, Russell, 25